C# For Beginners

A Step-by-Step Guide to Learn C#, Microsoft's Popular Programming Language

Julian James McKinnon

Table of Contents

Download the Audio Book Version of This Book for FREE

If you love listening to audio books on-the-go, I have great news for you. You can download the audio book version of this book for FREE just by signing up for a FREE 30-day audible trial! See below for more details!

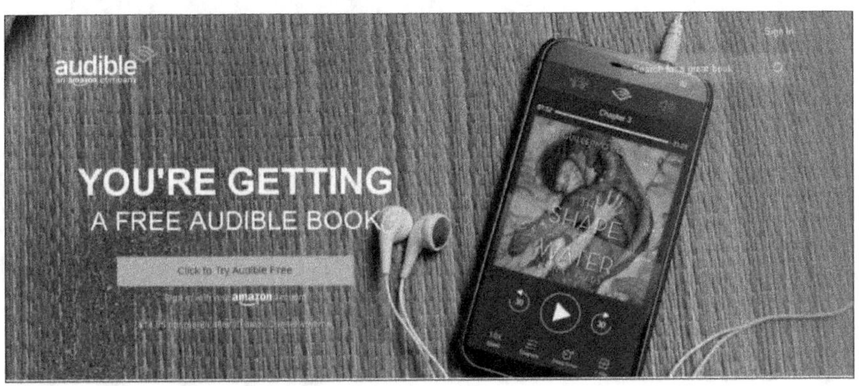

Audible Trial Benefits

As an audible customer, you will receive the below benefits with your 30-day free trial:

- FREE audible book copy of this book
- After the trial, you will get 1 credit each month to use on any audiobook
- Your credits automatically roll over to the next month if you don't use them
- Choose from Audible's 200,000 + titles
- Listen anywhere with the Audible app across multiple devices
- Make easy, no-hassle exchanges of any audiobook you don't love
- Keep your audiobooks forever, even if you cancel your membership
- And much more

Click the links below to get started!

For Audible US

For Audible UK

For Audible FR

For Audible DE

Introduction

Congratulations on purchasing ***C# for Beginners,*** and thank you for doing so.

The following chapters will discuss all of the things that you need to know to get started with the C# language.

There are a lot of different parts that come with this language, and being able to set it up well and ensure that you will be able to write some strong and powerful codes in the process is going to be a critical part of the whole process.

To start with our guidebook, we are going to take a closer look at what the C# language is all about.

We will talk about the benefits of working with this language, take a look at some of the software that we need to use to make this coding language work, and even look at some of the steps that we can take to write out our very first code in this language.

We will also look at this part so that we can learn how to set up the C# environment with all of the different parts that we need to make it happen.

When we are doing this kind of introduction, we will move on to some of the many parts that come with the C# language, and we will learn how we can utilize them for some of our own needs.

We will take a look at a few different options, including how to work with the C# variables, the importance, the different types of the operators in this language, and even how to go through and create some of our own conditional statements, which will ensure that our programs can make their own decisions, even if we are not there to help guide them with every possible input.

From there, we are going to spend some time looking at the steps that you can take to create your own objects, and define your own classes.

Both of these are important topics when it comes to working with an OOP language like C#; and we are going to spend our time exploring how to work with both and how they work together, including some codes to get it all done.

Another neat thing that we can do inside of this language, and that we will spend some time on in this guidebook is creating some of the necessary loops.

There are a wide variety of loops available, and we will discuss many of them, but they all help us to reduce the amount of space that our code takes up, can save a lot of time, and hold a bunch of information inside of a small amount of code.

We can then end this guidebook with a look at a few other important topics.

These include a look at the strings, lists, and arrays that are a big part of the code that you want to write as well.

These may seem like they are the same or very similar on the outside, but the more that you work with coding, the better you will need to understand them.

Then we can close out the discussion with a look at some of the best tips and tricks that a beginner programmer can use to help them see success with the C# language overall.

There are a lot of great options out there when it comes to coding languages that we can use, but none of them are going to provide us with the best frameworks, the best power, and all of the amazing features like we are going to see when it comes to using the C# language.

This guidebook took the time to explore more about this and how we can utilize it for our goals as well.

When you are ready to do more with the C# language, and you want to get started right away, make sure to check out this guidebook to help you out!

There are plenty of books on this subject on the market, thanks again for choosing this one!

Every effort was made to ensure it is full of as much useful information as possible.

Please, enjoy it!

Chapter 1: What is C#?

One of the neat things that you will enjoy when it comes to programming and all of the things that you can do with it is that there are actually quite a few different programming languages to choose from.

Each has been designed to handle a different kind of coding need, which can allow us to really specialize in the things that are the most important to us for our projects and our needs.

But one of the coding languages that we will spend some time on in this guidebook is known as C#.

Most people who are looking to get into coding, but have never done it in the past at all, will find that it is easy to be worried about the whole process when it is time for them to learn something new.

They know that coding is useful and can benefit them in a whole host of manners, but then they are worried that it is going to be too hard.

They could use it to create their own applications, websites, and programs, and it can even be the key that they need to open some new doors professionally.

But because of all the new options that are available when they work with this process, they are worried that it will be too hard to learn to code.

If you let the fear and the worry take over and you do not take the necessary time to learn one of these new languages, then, of course, the programming process, and the steps that are needed to work on them, are going to be pretty difficult for you to handle.

However, when it comes to finding a good language that you can work with, such as the simplicity and great features of the C# language, you will find that it is going to be so much easier to handle all of your projects whether you have learned how to do some programming in the past or this is your first step into the process.

With this in mind, it is time for us to dive in a little bit and learn some more about what is involved with the C# process, what we can do with this language that is so much better than some of the other options, and so much more!

Why Learn How to Use C#?

The first thing that we need to take a look at here is why we would want to learn how to work with the C# language.

There is a lot of other coding and programming languages out there that we can spend our time on, and many of them can provide us with the benefits that we need.

So then, why would we want to take the time to learn more about C# and how it can work for our needs as well?

As we mentioned a bit before, there are a ton of other coding and programming languages that we can pick out from, and each of them will work differently, providing us with some different benefits along the way.

Figuring out which one is going to be the right one for us is sometimes a challenge.

Some coders will pick out one based on how easy it looks, and others may decide to learn one because it can handle the specific tasks that they are looking at.

But you will find that no matter what your objective with coding is in the first place, working with the C# language is going to provide you with some benefits, ones that we are going to explore in this section.

Even though you are someone who is just beginning, knowing some of these benefits are going to help us to have more confidence in the coding language, and you will find that this is going to help us to really make some amazing programs and applications in the process.

Some of the benefits that we are going to see when it comes to the C# language includes:

1. The library with C# is larger than many other libraries, which gives you a lot more possibilities in the process.

   As a beginner, there are going to be a ton of parts of your code that may not come as easily as you would like without some practice.

   The good news is that the C# library is going to provide you some of the help that you need.

   You can add the necessary functions to the code without a ton of hassle in the process.

   You are even able to use them in a manner to make some changes to ensure your code is going to work in the way that you want.

2. It will get rid of the functions for you automatically.

   When you do some of your work with other coding languages, you will be the one responsible for removing the functions when they are done, all on your own.

This can be time-consuming and a hassle, especially if you end up missing a few of them.

One of the benefits that we will see with the C# language is that it is actually going to handle this work for you, making the whole process easier overall.

3. The C# language is an easy one to learn how to use for beginners.

   In fact, this is the language that most would consider the easiest out of all to learn how to code with.

   While there are going to be a few parts that add in some more complications to the mix, for the most part, you will find that you can recognize and use the different parts of the C# language with relative ease.

4. The C# language was originally designed to work with Windows, but it can also work on some of the other platforms that you decide as well.

   This language is going to work well with Linux, Mac, and Windows, as long as you make sure to download the .NET framework with it as well.

   Windows is often the preferred method to use with this language, though, since it comes with some additional products and features that help beginners use this language, so if you are still uncertain about the operating system you want to use, that would be the way to go.

5. The .NET framework is going to be your friend in this whole process and can make coding easier.

   This is going to be a program that is readily available on Windows computer systems, so you will not need to do additional work to get this one.

   However, it is also easy to install this on other operating systems, so that should not be a problem at all.

6. The C# language is going to share a lot of similarities to C++ and C languages.

   This is going to make it a lot easier for us to learn how to do the programming and some of the basics if you already know how to do some coding with this program.

   Even if you choose to just go with this language and not spread out to some of the others, you will find that the C# language has all of the power that you need to get the codes and programs done.

How to Get Started

Now that we know a bit more about some of the benefits that come with the C# language, it is time for us to take a look at some of the steps that are needed to get started.

One of the first things that we need to check before doing any coding is whether we have the .NET framework that we were talking about before because this will be the environment where we need to write out our own codes.

You should already have a kit for development that is found on a computer holding Windows if you are using that.

Starting with the Windows Vista version of the Windows operating system family, this is going to be a necessary framework to use, so you should find if the .NET framework is on your computer as long as you are up to that operating system or newer.

You will not need to download it since it is unlikely that your computer has an older system on it at this time.

However, if you are going through this process, and you find that your Windows computer does not have the .NET framework, or you are working with another operating system and it doesn't automatically come with this framework, then it is time to get to work.

For Mac and Linux, the Mono Project is going to be a bit easier to use and will work on these systems better than the .NET framework.

You can still find this at the Microsoft store, then just follow the instructions to get it to download for you.

You can also visit the website www.monoporject.com to get the download that is needed.

With the right framework in place, it is time for us to get started on some of the other things that we need to do with the C# language.

Assuming at this point that you have gone through and done all of the downloading that is necessary for the frameworks and programs that you really need, or you found that they were already on your system, it is time for us to get to work on using the C# language.

When we do some of this work on our Windows computer, you will find that the C# language is a simple one to work with.

The reason for this is that the Windows operating system is going to be compatible with our .NET framework automatically, and when we combine this with the fact that the C# language is a simple and flexible one to learn how to use, you can catch on to some of the codings in no time.

All of this is going to be there to help you while providing you with the necessary power to keep all of your codes strong.

For someone who is brand new to all of the ideas that we are talking about here when it comes to coding and programming, you will find that this language gives us the ease of use necessary while still providing us with all of the power to get our codes done.

Similar to what you will find when you work with many of the other coding languages out there, including options like Java, you will find that C# is not going to support things like code pointers.

And this is also not one of the languages that can support a process that is known as multiple inheritances.

We must remember some of this because they are things that some other coding languages can handle, and you don't want to be surprised by the lack of this later on.

You will find, though, that instead of offering some of these options, the C# language is going to provide you with a few other options, including type checking and memory collection.

Other important and powerful features are very noticeable from the C++ language that you can add to some of your codes based on what we would like to accomplish.

There are a lot of parts that we can utilize when it comes to working in the C# language, so let's dive into some of the actual codings and learn how this works so we can see some of these parts in action.

Writing Out a C# Program

With some of that background behind us, it is time for us to go through and actually see how we can write out our first program in C#.

This is the part that you have been waiting for.

We do not want to just hear a bunch of words about the language and nothing else, no actionable steps.

But that is why we are going to spend our time in this section, actually writing out one of the codes that we want to use in C#.

So, to get started with writing this code, the first thing that we need to accomplish is opening up our text editor so that we can get the C# language set up and ready to go.

If you are doing this on a device with Windows on it, then you just need to open up the Notepad to start.

There are other options that you can choose from, too, so make your decision before you work on the code and then get it installed and ready to go on your computer.

Once you have had a chance to open up your chosen editor, whether you are working with Notepad or another option, it is time to type in the following code to gain some of the practice that is necessary here:

```
class FirstProgram
{
static void Main()
{
        Console.WriteLine("Using C# is fun.");
        }
        }
```

Now you can access the command prompt and type:

```
    csc FirstProgram.cs
```

After you issue this command, the compiler for C# will process this file and then create a .exe file in the same location as your code.

For example, if you saved the original file on the desktop, you should see a new program come up called "FirstProgram.ee." right in the same place.

If there is an error in the code that you wrote, you will see an error message come up.

Now you can run this application by entering "FirstProgram.exe." into the command prompt.

If everything was done correctly, you should see that the command prompt will display the message: "Using C# is fun."

After you have had a chance to work with this program, it is time for us to actually take a bit of time and analyze the program and how it is supposed to work.

With the code that we worked on a bit above, we can see that it is actually a simple process to work with.

But even with all of the simplicity, we can find that there are a variety of parts and aspects of coding that had to come together to make this one work.

Some of the most important parts of the code above that we need to focus on include:

1. Take a look at the first line.

   This is the spot where we need to include a good identifier and a keyword.

   The keyword is going to be the main word that we find in the code that has a special function and can tell the compiler what action to take.

   With the keyword that is in our example, we are telling the compiler to create a new class for the program.

The identifier is then going to be in charge of listing out the variable, the class, and the method.

In that example, we are using one that is known as “FirstProgram”.

2. Then we can move on to the third line in the whole thing.

   This is where we are going to denote our Main() function.

   This is going to be the starting point of our application on the computer.

   When we have this, the program will be able to start by executing this kind of method regardless of where you decide to place it in your code.

   There will then be two words that can work in this method, including the void and static.

   These will then help us to determine what object is going to be found in the code.

3. Now we can skip to the fifth line.

   This is the final main part that we are going to see within the code that we wrote above.

   This is the line where we can write out some kind of message that should show up on the computer screen once you have executed the program.

The method that we are going to use here is the WriteLine() method so that the compiler knows that it is supposed to show the statement you're adding.

In addition to some of the different topics that we spent our time talking about above, some braces showed up in the code along the way.

These are going to also have some importance to the code that we want to write out because they are responsible for telling our computer that there are a lot of blocks of code that need to be separated throughout, and will help us to keep all of the parts nice and organized as we go along.

Chapter 2: How to Set Up the C# Language

While we did take some time to look at how to write some code in the C# language in the chapter above, we did get a little bit ahead of ourselves there.

Now it is time to back up the process a little bit and look at some of the basics that we need to know to learn how to set up the C# language completely so that it can work on our computers.

We will also take a look at how to work with the .NET Core and Visual Studio, and how these are going to combine together well on our program to give us the best results.

You will find in this process that when you can use the C# language that we are talking about here with the Visual Studio that we will introduce later, it is going to provide us with all of the necessary editing experience that we really need to make things work properly.

When we can add all of these features and benefits together with some good support that is present in C# IntelliSense, which is going to be what we use when writing outsmart code, and some help with the process of debugging, you will be off to a good start when it is time to write out our own codes.

Along the way, you will find that the C# language and some of the tools that are necessary to make it work are already found on a computer that has the Windows system on it.

This is a language that comes hand in hand with Windows, which is going to make things easier if you already have that system and plan to use it.

The great news is that this language is also able to work on the other two main operating systems but, keep in mind, it is going to take some extra work to get it over there, and sometimes the number of features you get when using C# on Mac or Linux will be limited.

However, even if your goal is to do the C# language on a Windows computer, it is important to go through the necessary steps to get Visual Studio installed with C#.

This Microsoft Visual Studio is going to be one of the options that you have for an integrated development environment or IDE, and it is already there from Microsoft for us to use.

It is often the best one to choose when you want to use C# for programming.

You also have to go through and do quite a bit of work to get all of the parts built up and ready to go for your program.

And you will find that even when it comes to the .NET platform, Visual Studio is going to be able to help.

It is going to be the one-stop-shop that we need for the applications that we are hoping to build up with this platform and this language, so it is worth our time to look into it a bit more.

With the help of Visual Studio, it is going to be a lot easier for us to get our applications to create, run, and go through the process of debugging as needed.

There are a few different types of applications that we can focus on here, including the forms-based and web-based, and they will all be options to develop on your IDE when you are ready.

The program of Visual Studio will be able to give us each feature that we need to get this part done.

With all of this information in mind, we need to take some time to look at the different steps that are necessary when we want to download and then install the Visual Studio IDE and use it for our needs.

When we get done with this installation, the IDE will be ready to go to get all of our programming needs done.

The simple steps that we can use to install the IDE will include:

1. You need to visit the Visual Studio website to download all of the files and other materials that you need.

   The websites that you can work with will include https://www.visualstudio.com/downloads/

a. You can choose to go with the Community or the Professional Edition.

   The first one is going to be free, but the second is going to cost a bit.

   We are going to take a look at how to install the professional edition here because it is the one that has more of the features that you are looking for.

2. When you pick your version, you need to click on the downloaded .exe file.

3. When you get to the next screen, make sure that you click on continue.

4. At this point, we are going to start with some of the downloading processes that we need with Visual Studio.

   This is going to include all of the initial files that you need.

   Keep in mind that the download speed is going to vary based on your own internet connection and how fast it can handle the work.

5. We are then going to get a new screen to come up for us.

   You will need to click install on the version of the Visual Studio IDE that you would like to work with.

6. At this point, we are going to head on over to the next screen, which is where we are going to find a ton of options to choose from.

   Our goal here is to select the .NET desktop development option, and then we can go through the installation process to get that on our desktop computer before coding.

7. The following step is where Visual Studio can spend a bit of time downloading the files that you need based on those other selections that we made above.

   You can just click on the parts we suggested, or you can go through and add in some customizations if you would like as well.

8. Once we are done getting that download going, the computer is going to require that you go through and reboot your computer.

   This has to be done to get everything in place, so agree to work on that and let the computer restart.

9. After the reboot is all done, which can take a few minutes to accomplish, it is time to open the computer up and then look around for the Visual Studio IDE that we just worked on.

   You can then open this IDE up to use it:

a. When we have it opened up, we should be able to pick out the theme that we want to use here.

   This is not going to matter too much, and you can pick out the one that you personally like for your coding.

b. When you have made your selection, you can then click on continue with Visual Studio to get started.

10. When we get to the IDE that works with Visual Studio, you can then navigate around a bit and find the File Menu.

    You then need to click on that menu, then look for the part that says "create a new C# application" and click on that.

11. You are then able to go through all of the necessary steps to get this part of the process done.

    When all of the steps are done, you will easily be able to write out the different codes that you want to use with the C# language without issues.

Now, you will notice that there are a ton of reasons why you would want to spend your time working with this particular IDE over some of the others.

Yes, a quick search will show you that there are other options that you can choose from, but none of them will provide us with the same kinds of features at all.

For example, this Visual Studio IDE is going to make it easier for us to create choice applications in any of the different languages that rely on our .NET framework.

This adds in a bit more versatility to your needs.

It is also an IDE that will make it helpful to create all of the types of applications that we want here.

For someone who is just starting out with coding and learning the ropes a little bit, the IDE from Visual Studio is a great option to help debug some of your codes as well.

There are always going to be times when your code will run into some issues, and being able to debug it will ensure that it works in the manner that you would like.

When we use the Visual Studio IDE, it allows us to test out some of the applications that we are using at the same time that we try to build them up.

This is going to save us a ton of time and will allow for a kind of learning on the job process so that we can get better with some of the codings we want to do as well.

You will find that all of the cool extensions that come with this will make it a lot more fun to learn how to work with this coding language overall.

While there may be a lot of options out there to help us learn C#, you will find that the IDE that comes with Visual Studio is going to be one of the best options to choose, and if you can go through a few of the steps that are in this chapter, you will have it all downloaded and set up so that you can actually work on some of the codings you would like.

Chapter 3: How to Work with the Variables

When it comes to doing some work with your chosen coding language, it is important to learn a bit about the variables and what we can do with them.

These are important, no matter which coding language you want to learn, so we are going to take a bit of time to learn more about them and how they can work for our needs.

Now that we have the whole C# language set up and ready to go on any computer we want to use, it is time for us to go through and actually take a good look at the variables that work on this, as well as the other data types that we can use as well.

All of these are going to work in a slightly different manner from one another, so we need to learn what they are about and what we can do with them.

While some of the different things that you can do with these variables can be considered more advanced and can add in some more complications to the process, you will find that these variables are also a part of the basics of this language, and the basic idea that comes with this is simple to learn.

We have already taken a look at a good example of a code that we can write in C#, so now let's see how we can use the variables to help us write out our codes a bit more in-depth.

The Different Types of Data

The first thing that we have to explore when it comes to our variables includes all of the different types of data that are found with the C# language.

When you work with this, you can divide it up into two main parts, ones that are different but can also work well together.

These are going to be separated out into "the value type" and "the reference type."

When we look a bit more closely at the value types, you have to remember that the data has to be passed over the method that you plan to use here.

But, if you are working with the reference type of these, then we have to make sure that we add about our method as the value is something that we will place in another location in the code.

Some of the types of data that we can utilize include:

- Ulong
- Double
- Long

- Float
- Uint
- Int
- Ushort
- Sbyte
- Short
- Byte
- Bool—when you use this type, the values that you are allowed to store can only be two.

  The values are going to be false and true, so it is good for conditional statements and logical expressions.
- Decimal
- Char—this is a data type that is only allowed to have one single character.

  When you are writing the char value, you must include it with single quotes such as writing out 't' 'b' and so on.

The C# Variables

You will find that no matter how much code you write, there will come the point when you will need to go through and execute the codes.

When it is time to execute the code, the computer program is going to hold onto the data until it is time to execute it again.

The best way that we can store this information is to use the variables.

To make this as easy as possible, a variable is going to reserve a spot in the memory of our computers to hold onto the data that you try to create.

Because of these facts, the variables are going to have at least one value attached to them, and sometimes more than one value at a time.

And this value will then be saved over to that reserved spot in the memory where we held onto the variable.

When you work with this language, we can use the syntax to help you create a new variable:

<data_type> <name_of_variable>

When you type in the above code to your compiler, you are creating a variable that will save a part of the memory so that you can store a value there.

The programmer will then be able to access this variable using the identifier it was given.

For example, if you had listed the formula above as char x, you would be able to find the variable by bringing up x.

C# is unique in that it is going to help us to initialize some of the variables that we want to use when it is time to declare them.

This term is going to refer to the process of placing a value on the variable when you create it.

You simply need to use one of the assignment operators, and the operator that we need here is simply the equal sign.

Then you can write out the value that you want to place there when this is all done.

Another thing that we can do here is to declare a few variables at a time in the same statement, as long as we are working with the same type of data.

We just need to make sure that each of the entries that we add to that statement has a comma in between to help separate them out.

While we are here, though, we need to make sure that the variable is declared before we try to access them and use them in our code again.

The C# language is also going to make it so that we must implement a new rule, which we will know as a definite assignment.

What this means is that you will need to take a bit of programming time initializing the local variables you want to use before they are ever added to some of the code that you write.

Then you can go through and assign the initial value of our local variable while you declare it, using the process that we were just talking about in the process.

One note to keep in mind here is that when we are working through this phase and using this language, the variable we will use will be named using this method as well because the values that the variables should hold onto will actually change each time that you execute and run that program.

The changes will happen in your values, but what they change into will really depend on what you want them to be to make the code work.

How to Create an Identifier

One thing that is nice about Microsoft is that it is going to provide you with a variety of suggestions that you can use to get C# to work well.

And one of these recommendations is that programmers of C# should work with the Camel notation with their work and with the variables that they write out.

Then, when you work with the methods we have talked about, you will need to work with the method that is a bit different, one known as "the Pascal notation".

To a beginner, this may not make sense, so let's dive into them.

When we talk about the Camel notation, you will need to make sure that the first letter in the variable name is a lower case.

If your new identifier or variable is going to be a compound word, then you will need the first letter in the second word to be an uppercase letter.

This helps to keep them separate and tends to make reading them a bit easier.

A good example of some of the codes that we can write out in camel case would be the following:

payment complete payment

mathematics firstclass

The Pascal notation will take things a bit differently.

This notation style is going to ask you to start the first word using an uppercase letter.

The first letter in all of the other words in the sequence should also be done in uppercase as well. Some examples using the Pascal notation include:

WriteLine() ReadLine()

Start() Main()

While you are naming these identifiers, you will be able to work with numbers and underscores as well.

But you will not be able to start these identifiers with a number.

You can write out something like sevenbooks, but you could not write out 7books.

We need to remember when we work on this that the notations are not something that is required all the time, and you can make some changes to use them to help us give the identifiers a name if you would like.

But the Pascal and Camel notations are going to be seen as the proper way to do it in coding, so it is best to use it so that other programmers know what you are talking about along the way.

As we can see, already working with the C# language is not that hard to work with, even as a beginner.

There are going to be quite a few parts that come together that we need to remember as we go through, and sometimes it is going to seem like a lot to try and keep track of with all of the rules.

But as we go through our coding, we will see why these parts are in place, and why they are so important to some of the work that we want to do with our own codes as well.

Chapter 4: Handling the C# Operators

It is hard to have a good discussion about the C# language if we don't take the time to talk about the operators and how these are supposed to work in some of our codes.

These are a relatively simple option that we can handle, but they are going to be important and can really make sure that our codes work well. In fact, we even took some time to talk about one of the operators, the assignment operators, in the last chapter about variables.

These operators are going to show up all over the place in our codes, so it is time to learn what they are, what they mean, and how we can use them.

There are a few different types of operators that we can add to our code, and each one is going to have its own role to play in the process.

No matter how you end up using these in the codes you write out, they will all have their own job to handle as well.

When we add in the right operators, we will be able to add in some of the functionality that we want as well.

These operators are going to be easier to handle than you may think, but the functionality and the power that comes with them are going to be amazing.

The neat thing here is that no matter which of the other coding languages you want to work with, whether you handle the C# language or another option, these operators are going to be really important to work with.

We are going to take some time in this chapter to look at the different types of operators and how we can work with each one.

Using the Arithmetic Operators

When you are ready to work with the operators, the first one that we need to talk about is the arithmetic operators.

These are going to be pretty simple to work with, and if you have been able to take any math classes in the past, then you are going to have a good familiarity with how these works, and you will know how to work with these pretty quickly.

When we handle some of these arithmetic operators, you will find that they are going to be in charge of telling the computer to work on a few of these functions as well.

As long as you can remember the right symbol with these, and you place the numbers all in the right order and use this well, then the arithmetic functions are going to be able to work out the way that we want.

Some of the most popular arithmetic operators that you can use when handling the C# language will include:

- "+" this is the addition operator.

  It is going to add two operands together.

  So, you would get x+y=25

- "-" this is the subtraction operator.

  It is going to allow you to subtract the value of the right-handed operand from the left-hand operand.

  So, you would get y-x=-5.

- "*" this is the one that will tell the computer to multiply the two operands.

  So, you could do x*y=150.

- "/" this one is the operator that will tell the computer to divide the left-hand operand with the right-hand operand.

  For example, y/x.

- “%” is often called the remainder of the modulo operator.

  It is going to divide the left-hand operand by the right operand and then returns the remainder.

- “++” is the increment operator.

  It is going to increase the value of the operand by one.

  So, you would have ++x=16

- “—” programmers will often call this the decrement operator.

  It is going to decrease the value of the operand by one.

  This means that you will have –x=14.

You will find that there are a lot of times when you will be able to work with these arithmetic operators, and they are fairly easy to pull out and use.

They can also be there to help out in codes where you would like to take two numbers or statements in the code and do some kind of mathematical formula on them as well, such as addition or subtraction.

You have to remember to use the order of operations with these, though, to make sure that the code is going to behave in the manner that you want.

If you need a little refresher about the order of operations and how it works, it is the method that tells us which order we need to have the numbers to do the math correctly and get the answer that we want.

Remember that, going left to right, we need to do all of the multiplication, then all of the division, after that all of the addition, and finally the subtraction.

If you do not use this when you do the work in C#, then the answer will be wrong.

Using the Assignment Operators

Now that we have had some time to look a bit more at the options that you can use with the arithmetic operators, it is time for us to move on and look at the second kind of operator that will work well in C#, and that is the Assignment operators.

The assignment operators are going to be the ones that we will use when we want to assign a value to our variable, or some other similar method along the way.

Think back to the variables that we already spent some time on.

The variables, and other parts of our identifiers along the way, need to get a value to be assigned over to them.

If not, then you are just reserving blank spots in the memory of your computer.

And the assignment operator is going to make sure that you can assign that value over to it and get everything to go through the right way.

The most common of these types of operators, as you can guess, is going to be the equal sign.

These operators are going to be responsible for making sure that the value can go right to the variable that you want.

But there are other operators that we can use here that fit under this category.

A few of the other assignment category operators that you may recognize when you work with this language and do some of the codings we will explore later on, include:

- "=" this operator will allow you to perform simple assignment operations.

  It is going to assign the value to a variable that you are working on at that time.

  For example, writing *int sample = 100* will tell the program that you want to assign 100 to the variable that is called "sample".

  It won't perform any extra processes on this variable or the value involved.

- "+=" this is the additive assignment operator.

  It is going to add up the values of your two operands and then will assign the sum to your left-hand operand.

- "-=" programmers will often refer to this as the subtractive assignment operator.

  It is going to subtract the value of the operand on the right side from the one on the left side, and then assign the difference to the left-hand operand.

- "*=" this operator will multiply the values of each operand, and then will assign the product to the left-hand operand.

- "/=" this is when you will divide up the two variables, and then take the result and assign it to the variable on the left.

When you want to work with one of the above assignment operators, it is important to double-check that both of your operands are actually the same type of data.

You will find that, in some cases, the operands being different means that they are not going to be compatible with one another, and if you try to work with these, then your program will not behave in the way that you would like.

So, check on this part of the code so that you don't end up with an error that you have to try and fix later on.

Using the Relational Operators

Next on our list of operators is going to be the kind known as the relational operators.

Remember that the arithmetic operators we talked about above are responsible for helping us do any kind of mathematical equations that we want inside of the codes, and then the assignment operators are responsible for making sure that all of our variables, or some of the spaces that are reserved in the memory of our computer, will have a good value assigned to them.

But now it is time to shift our focus for a moment and look at how these relational operators work.

First, the relational operators are going to be the best to work with because they can help us have a chance to compare the values of two different operands in the code.

Because we can make this happen, these are going to be the best to use when we handle some of our conditional statements later on.

There are several relational operators that we can use in this language.

To make it easier and to really see what is going to happen when we use these, we have to assume from the beginning that d = 100 and e = 150:

- "==" this is the operator that you can use to check the equality of two values.

  If the two values end up being equal, the operand will tell you it is true. Otherwise, the operand will tell you it is false.

  For example, saying the d == e would show up as false.

- "!=" this operator allows you to test the inequality of two values.

  If the values end up not being equal, it will tell you this is true.

  For example, e != d would result in true.

- ">" this operator is used to check whether the operand on the left is greater than the operand on the right.

  If it is, then the operator will tell you it is true.

  For example, saying that e > d would be true.

- "<" this is the less than an operator, it will allow you to check whether the operand on the left side is less than the operand on the right side.

If it is, you will get it to show up true, such as the formula d < e.

- “>=” this is the operand that will say it is true if the value of the operand on the left side is greater than, or equal to the operand on the right side.

  Otherwise, it will tell you the statement is false.

  For example, saying that e >=d evaluates as true.

- “<=” with this operator, you will get a true response if the operand on the left side is less than, or equal to the operand that is on the right side.

  For example, d <= e is true.

One of the things that we need to remember when we work with this particular type of operator is that you will actually end up with a result that is Boolean each time that you want to use them.

What this means is that you will get an answer that is either true or false based on the conditions that you add to that part of the code.

At this time, it is a good idea for us to go through and check the code, seeing whether we add in the proper number of equal signs to make this work.

If we are doing the equality operator, there need to be two equal signs; otherwise, we are working with the assignment operator, and that will get us a different result than what we want at this time with all of this.

Using the Logical Operators

We can take a look at the next type of operator that is important for some of our work, which is known as the logical operators.

This one, similar to how we are going to work with some of the other Boolean values, is going to accept and then rely on the idea of true and false when we work with them in our code.

When we are taking a look at some of the logical operators that you would like to add to the code, you will find that, for the most part, we will focus on four main choices.

We are going to take a look at these below, but to make this easier, assume that c and d will be true and that e is false:

- "&&" this operator is called logical AND.

  It will only result in true if both operands are true.

  For example, d && c will evaluate it as true.

- "||" this is the logical OR.

  This operator is going to give you a true response if at least one of your operands is true. For example, c || e will result in true.

- "^" this operator is the Logical Exclusive OR, and it will result in a true if one of the operands is true.

  If both operands can be false or true, the operator will give you a false.

- "!" with this one, you will be able to reverse the value of your Boolean variable.

  For example, if you type in !d, you will get a false.

Using the Bitwise Operators

Now it is time to move on to the final operator that we will discuss in this guidebook, and these will be known as the bitwise operators.

This is a type of operator that we can use, and at first glance, it is going to seem like it is the same thing as the logical operators that we already talked about.

The main difference that you will see between these bitwise operators and the previous logical operators is that the bitwise options are going to take a value only if it is binary, and then turn it into something that is a Boolean result.

These are going to be values that will represent true or false, but they will come out as a 0 or 1, and then we can see these come as the output in the whole process.

These binary values are sometimes going to be difficult to work with overall because a lot of non-programmers will not understand how these are supposed to work in some of the codes that they want to write.

Let's take a look at an example of some of the different bitwise operators that you can work with to see how they can be handled here.

For this, let's assume that I = 0, h = 1, j =0 and g = 1

- "&" this is the operator that is known as the Bitwise AND.

  It is going to assign 1 to the positions where both of the operands have 1.

  For example, g & h will give you 1.

- "|" this is the bitwise OR.

  It is going to assign 1 to the positions when there is at least one of the operands with a 1.

  For instance, doing h | 1 will give you a result of 1.

- "^" this is the exclusive OR that will work well for binary data.

  Just like working with the logical values, this kind of operator is only going to give you 1 in the areas that the operand has a 1.

For example, if you do g^j you will get a result of 1.

The bitwise operator is going to be a bit more work when it comes to the different operators that we can work with.

And there are not necessarily a lot of times when we would want to bring out this kind of operator in the codes that we are going to do.

But this is a good option to work with and know about so we can see how this is going to work when we do need it.

You will find that all of these categories of operators will be important to the codes that we want to write along the way.

They are all a bit different and can handle things differently as you go, but they can still help you get a lot done and see some good and powerful results in the codes that you want to write.

Take some time to study these and see how they work, so that you can add them to your own codes quickly and efficiently.

Chapter 5: Teaching Your C# Programs to Make Decisions

In this chapter, it is time to get into some of the fun stuff that we can do when it comes to writing out our own codes.

In particular, we are going to learn a bit more about the conditional statements, or the decision control statements and how we can make these work for our needs.

There are a lot of times when we will create a program that needs to take in input from the user.

We can't always guess what input the user is going to provide us.

So, we can use these conditional statements and set them up with a condition on how we want them to respond to different potential inputs, and then have the program behave in the right manner based on these conditions.

There are times when you are working with your programs, and you want to make sure that it can handle some decision-making on its own.

You can have it all set up, with the right conditions, ahead of time, and then the code can respond based on the user input that it receives as well.

The computer program is going to behave in the manner that you want, even if you have no idea what the input is, without you having to make a lot of guesses.

You will find that there are actually a couple of different types of conditional statements that you can work with, and the choice you make is going to depend on how you want the code to behave.

Each of these conditional statements will allow us to work in different situations, but it often depends on how many features and how much decision-making you would like the program to do.

We will take a look at some of these through this chapter so you can see what we mean here, and learn a bit more about how all of this will come together.

As we mentioned, there are several types of conditional statements we can choose from, rather than just one, and each can handle the information that it receives as an input in a different manner.

This helps us to make sure that we get the right decision out of the code, doesn't matter how the user provides us with input.

The options of conditional statements that we can work within our C# language include:

The If Conditional Statement

To start our journey in the world of conditional statements, we need to handle the if statement.

This is going to be seen as one of the most basic out of all the conditional statements, and you will see how it sometimes lacks in the amount of functionality that we need when it comes to these statements.

There are not a lot of times when we will use the if conditional statement on its own, but it still gives us some practice with how this works, and what we can do with it so that we will spend a bit of time here.

When we are ready to write out one of these if statements, we need to make sure that the code is only going to need to provide the user with a specific reply if the input that is given matches up to all of the conditions that you set in the code to start with.

If the input does match with the conditions, then the code is going to execute, and often, it provides some kind of message to the user.

You can also choose to have it go through and execute something else if this works better for your type of code.

When we use the if statement, you will only end up with a response or an output if the input that the program is provided matches up with the conditions that are in the code.

If the user gives the wrong input, based on the conditions, then the code will not execute the next part of the code.

It doesn't have another part of the code to tell it how to behave, if a statement can recognize at this point, is whether the condition is met or not.

Since it is not met, it will not execute the message or the part that you add in there.

The good news that we are going to find here is that setting up the if statement is going to be a lot easier to accomplish than you may think in the beginning.

A good way to see how if the statement can work is to look at the code example that we have below:

```
If (x > 0)
        {
        Console.Write("The value is positive.");
        }
```

With the example that we listed above, certain things need to happen.

If the value that the user puts in is higher than zero, then the program is set up to print off "The value is positive".

However, if the expression turns out to be false, or the input is less than zero, then the program will ignore the whole statement that comes after Console.

Write and will move on.

The If-Else Statement

As we discussed a bit in the above section, there are going to be a few issues that can show up when we try to work with the if statement.

There are a lot of situations in coding, even as a beginner when these are going to be difficult to use and won't get the work done that we want.

For example, it is usually not a good idea in our codes to set up any potential that the program will not act at all if the input is wrong.

You want to make sure that no matter what the user adds in as their input, even if it is considered wrong by the code that you are working with, some kind of result will still show up so they know that they did it wrong, or some other indication.

The choice you make here is going to depend on how your code runs.

This is exactly why we are going to stop here and look at the second kind of conditional statement that we can use in our codes.

This one is known as the if-else statement.

This is going to add in a ton of power to the code; any code that you are writing, and can make it possible for us to have two, three, and more options to base the input of the user on.

You can technically use as many of these options as you would like in the if statement, but the idea is that it is set up in a manner that will help us to make sure that everything gets an answer.

A good syntax that we can use to help us understand how the if-else statement is going to work includes:

If (the Boolean expression)

{The statement/s you want to run if the result is true;

}

Else

{The statement/s you want to run if the result is false;

}

As we can see with the code that we wrote above, there is going to be a lot of power that we can get with the if-else statement.

This is going to be a basic option when it comes to using the if-else statement, but it is simple to go through and add in some more lines and more conditions to add in the power that you need here.

With these statements, if the answer is found to be false, then the code simply skips the first condition and goes on to the second part to see if that one is true or not.

If there happens to be more than two options, then this process continues until we reach the else statement of it.

If the input did not match up with all of the other parts, then it will automatically match up with the else part of the statement, and that is the condition that is met.

That part of the code will execute for us to ensure that something shows up on the screen in the process.

Now that we know a bit more about how the if-else statement is supposed to work for our needs, it is time for us to take a closer look at how this is going to work using an actual example to ensure that it behaves in the manner that we want.

A good example of how we can use this will include:

```
If ( x > o)
    {
    Console.Write("This value will be positive.");
    }
    Else
        {
        Console.Write("The value is less than or equal to
zero.")
        }
```

You will find that in the example that we did above, the else clause is going to be hidden, at least until the Boolean expression turns out to be false.

It is going to be there when, and if the process really requires it, or if the value comes out as false for that situation.

But if the value is true and matches up with the conditions that you add to the code, then you will find that the first statement is going to be the one that we will use.

You will find that there are a lot of situations where you will want to bring out the if-else statement in your C# code, but it may seem a bit complex to work with as a beginner.

Take some time to practice some of the codes that we have above to ensure that you get to experience typing in these codes and that it is going to match up with how you want to write your codes out as well.

The Nested Conditional Statements

Something a little bit unique when we work with our conditional statements in C# is the idea of the nested conditional statements.

These are going to be where we can take two of the statements that we already talked about above, and we are going to combine them together to make them into a nested conditional statement.

So, we can take one if statement and put it inside one of our other if statements.

This is going to add another level of complexity to what we are doing in our statements and can help us to really make our programs work hard.

If this is the kind of conditional statement that you would like to work with, you need to remember that if you do write one out and end up with an error or a mistake, it is going to take a long time to fix it.

Whether the mistake happens near the beginning, at the end, or somewhere in between, if it is there, it is going to cause an error in the whole thing, and you have to take some time to fix it, or the code will not work.

This takes some time and can be frustrating for a beginner who is trying to make this work.

Another thing to consider with these nested conditional statements is that you are technically able to go through and add in as many levels to this one as you would like.

However, as a beginner, it is probably best to not go above three levels, and two is often plenty for the codes that you want to write out as well. If you do go above three levels with these kinds of conditional statements, then you may end up with some coding that is harder to handle and may not work in the manner that you want.

This is a good rule to stick with as a beginner to help make coding a bit easier.

While this seems complex, and you may assume right off the bat that your codes would not need these nested statements, there are some situations where it will come up, and it is a cool piece of programming to learn how to do whether you use it or not.

A good example of how we can write out some good code with the nested conditional statement is found below:

```
Double r = 60;

Double s = 70;

If (r ==s)

{

        System.Console.WriteLine("These numbers are equal.);

        }

        Else

        {

                If (r > s)

                System.Console.WriteLine("The value of the first variable is greater than that of the second one.")'

                }

                Else

                {

                        System.Console.WriteLine(The value of the second variable is greater than that of the first one.")'

                }

        }
```

With the example that we are looking at above, you will have a few options that will work with the if-else clause.

This will allow you to pick out the command so that the program knows what it needs to readout.

This will help you to do some more with your program and will make it easier to make the program more complicated.

There are a lot of different times when you will want to work with these conditional statements in your C# code.

These will help you add in some more interaction between your code and whoever is using your program.

It is simple to work with, but will ensure that you can make a complex code in your program.

Chapter 6: Creating Objects in C#

C# is considered one of the OOP languages.

This means that we are working with an object-oriented programming language, one that is going to be based on objects and classes as part of its organization.

This is going to be a simple topic that we can handle and work with, but it is also important to learn more about and see why it matters, and what it will mean to some of the codes that we will try to handle along the way.

Without these classes and the objects that they contain, the organization that we want to maintain and rely on inside of the C# language is going to be impossible.

This is why we need to understand more about the OOP languages, and why we are going to take some time to look at the necessary steps to help us create these classes and objects in our own codes as well.

Let's dive in and see what we can do with all of this.

The C# Classes and Objects

To help us get started on all of this, the first step is that we have to spend some of our time talking about what the objects are, and how the C# language is going to use them to execute codes.

Programming is something that has really seen some big changes since it first began, which has ensured that programmers are going to work with a lot of different methods to help them create some of the new applications their programs and computers need.

One of the best upgrades to happen to these programming languages is the object-oriented programming, or OOP, that we are talking about with C# and other similar languages.

In fact, most of the modern coding languages out there are going to rely on this because it ensures that your coding is easy to use and understand, and it will help us to code better as a beginner.

You will find that there are a ton of components that your coding needs to be able to handle and make a code behave.

But the OOP part of our language is going to help us break all of these parts up into more manageable chunks so that nothing gets lost and it all will behave in the manner that it should.

Since there is the fact that there are a ton of aspects that we need to have to go with one another to ensure this process works and our program will perform well, we need to divide some of these components up a bit and then learn a bit more about what they are going to do.

Let's look at the idea of these OOP languages, the classes, the objects, and so much more to see how this will work for us.

The Basics of the OOP Language

The very first thing that we need to understand when we come here is what the OOP language is going to mean, and why this is so important to what we are doing in our coding.

To keep it simple, OOP is basically just a style of coding that is going to rely on objects, ones that are actually created by the programmer and can relate back to some of the physical objects that we find in the world around us all of the time.

These OOP languages are nice because they can provide us with the exact model that we need to work with based on how we want to use our objects, and they can also be based on how we would like to work with these objects in the real world as well.

If you have a ball in your coding, then it is going to look, feel, and act in the same manner as a ball would in the real world.

When we compare this to some of the other languages that you can use for coding, you would have to spend your time on these working with more abstract ideas.

Abstract ideas are hard to work with, and that made it hard for beginners to even understand what was going on in the code, much less use it in a manner that they could code properly.

This was the only way to do things when coding started, but it set the bar too high for a lot of people to get into the world of coding, and most felt defeated and stopped before they even had a chance to get started.

On the other hand, the OOP languages took this challenge away and made things easier.

With these, you get the benefit of throwing out some of those abstract ideas and instead, had them set up so that you could work with objects that are easier to handle and understand as well.

And most of the modern coding languages out there rely on this process now, which can make life easier for you as a beginner.

The Objects

Now that we know a bit more about how these OOP languages are supposed to work, and what they can do to make coding easier for everyone, it is time to look a bit more at some of the objects that make up this type of language.

Programmers can work with these objects in any manner that they want.

These digital objects are going to be there to represent some of the physical objects that you want to find in your code.

When you work with any of the modern OOP languages, which includes C#, you have to keep in mind though that the objects need to have a few key characteristics in place to work well.

These characteristics are going to include:

- State—this is the characteristic that will define the object.

  These can be general or specific.

- Behavior—this is the characteristic that will declare all the actions that an object can do.

A good method to use to make sure that we are better able to understand how these are meant to work is to look at an example of this.

Let's say that we want to add a ball to our code.

The state of this ball is going to be.

Things like what the ball is made from, the size of the ball, and the color of the ball.

We could even talk about how the ball feels when we hold it.

On the other hand, when we are talking about the behavior of the ball, we would focus more on the things that the ball can do.

This could include things like the ball rolling, the ball bouncing, kicking the ball, throwing the ball, and so on.

Any time that we want to work with one of these types of languages, we will find that it is easy to combine the information and the technique, and then you can process them as the same thing.

The programming object is then going to have time to match up to how it is supposed to behave and look when it would be in the real world, and then it will go through and hold onto all of this information and these actions to use later when the code actually executes.

These objects are going to be an important part of the code that we want to write.

We will use a lot of objects along the way, and as we will see here in a moment, the classes that we can create will come in and provide us with all of the storage that we need, ensuring that these objects stay together and are easy to find at the right parts of the code.

The Classes

The next thing that we need to take a look at concerning these is the classes.

While we are on this topic, looking at some of the objects and how they are supposed to work, it is time for us to go through and look a bit more at the classes and how these will relate to some of the objects we work with, and what this will mean to our coding language.

To start, when we work with the C# language, the classes are going to be the part that helps define the characteristics of the objects we did before and can help us to hold onto all of these for organizational purposes.

These classes are nice because they will be responsible for helping us to have a structure or a model to base things on, making it easier to effectively define the nature of any object that our classes are supposed to hold.

The classes are going to be considered part of the foundation of what is needed to make the OOP language work well, and then they are directly linked back to the object that goes with it.

They will allow us to put in as many objects as we want to it, sometimes even a collection, so that they work well with one another.

So, this brings us to the part of needing to dive in a bit more to see how these classes are going to work in our code.

The example that we are going to look at here is going to be a new class that we name Toys, and then the object that we want to put into this specific class is going to be known as Ball.

With this particular instance, the ball is going to be just one of the instances that are found in the Toy class that we are creating.

However, the Toy class is going to help us out with this one because it helps to define the behavior and the state of not just the object of the ball, but with any of the other toys that we try to put into that class as well.

In addition to the ball object, we can go through and add in things like a bike, a doll, a dinosaur, or something else.

These objects could be defined by our class at the same time.

How to Create Classes in C#

With some of the information that we discussed above, it is time for us to take this a bit further and actually create one of our own classes in this language.

After we have had a chance to work on some of our own codes, and we bring in the “class” keyword, it is time for us to go through and actually indicate to the identifier what you would like to see.

This has to be done along with some of the variables and the different methods that you are hoping to use so that the class will work.

We, of course, want to get the power behind this while keeping it as simple as possible.

To make sure that this happens, we have to use all of the right parts and ensure that they are in order.

Some of the parts that are necessary when creating our classes include:

- Fields—these are any of the variables that will belong to a particular data type.
- Methods—you can use these methods to manipulate the data

- Properties—in this language, the properties are going to enhance how well the fields work.

  The property will provide some extra management abilities for the information and give it to the fields.

At this point, it will probably be easier if you take a look at how to work with the classes, and how to make sure that they do what you would like.

We are going to now take a look at an example of how this code will work and the different theories that have been going on with it.

Here we are going to use "book" as the name of the class, and then it will have the properties of size and type.

The example that you can use is as follows:

```
Public class Book

{

        Private string BookType:

        Private string size;

        Public string BookType

        {

        Get
```

```
{
Return this. BookType;
}
Set
{
        This. BookType = value'
}
}
        Public string Size
        {
                Get
                {
                Return this size;
                }
                Set
                {
                this.size = value;
                }
```

}

public Book()

{

this.bookType = "Dictionary";

this.size = "large";

}

public book(string bookType, string size)

{

this.bookType = bookType;

this.size = size;

}

public void Sample()

{

Console.WriteLine(" Is this a {0},

BookType):

Now that we have had some time to create one of our own classes, it is time to go through and create some of our own objects as well.

We need to fill up some of the classes with these objects so that it actually has a purpose inside of the codes that we are writing here.

And that is exactly what we are going to spend our time doing now.

Once we have been able to go through and create the classes that we did above, it is time for us to go through and create a few objects that are going to work in our codes and can go right into our classes.

Creating our own objects is not going to be all that difficult to work with, so we are going to take some time to look at all of the steps that we can take to make this happen, and what we can do to help create an object, whether it is just one or many, for our code to work.

With some of these thoughts in mind, the first thing that we need to focus on here is learning how we can create one of the necessary objects inside one of the classes that we created above.

To help us get started, we need to go through and make up a new keyword to get going here.

Usually, the programmer will start out by assigning a new object to their variable to ensure that it becomes the same data type as the class you want it in.

Remember that doing this is not going to help us copy the object to the variable that we wish to use, but it is going to be useful when we want to have a reference for the variable to the object that we assigned to it.

To help make sure that we understand how to do this, take a look at the code below:

```
Book someBook = new Book()
```

This is a good example that you can use because it is going to take the instance of a book and assign it over to the variable that we named someBook.

This will ensure that the proper object is going to the right class as is needed.

Then we can take a look at some of the system's classes that are going to be important to the work that we are doing.

Sometimes in this language, you will find that a feature that we can enjoy is the library that comes with it.

This library is going to include many of the classes that you need automatically; including the console, string, and math, so that we can use them as a default.

As you go through and write out some more of these codes, just remember that the .NET framework that comes with it is set up to work well with the C# library, so using it should not be a problem.

While we are on this topic, you will fall in love with how easy it is to use the .NET framework to get the job done for you.

This is because the library that you want to use with the C# language is going to work just fine with this framework, and you will find that they get along well and don't run into a lot of troubles.

These classes that you use are helpful as a beginner, especially if you have never had a chance to work with programming in the past at all.

One thing that we do need to note here, though, is that when you are working with these classes, they will go through the process of hiding the logical implementations.

You still need to focus on what the classes are going to do for you, rather than having to worry about all of the mechanics about how they get the work done.

Because of this fact, the classes that have been built-in with the C# language are not going to be out there in the open for everyone to see.

You simply need to go through and use these codes for general purposes rather than the mechanics of things.

Giving the Object a Parameter

Another topic that we need to spend some time on in the C# language is how we can make sure we assign the right parameters to the object.

This language is going to make it easier to assign the parameters that you want to any object, as long as it is one that you have already created.

This is actually a pretty easy method to use, and you can add parameters to any of the objects that are in your code.

The right syntax that we can work with to assign these parameters, or any parameters that you want to the object, will include:

Book someBook = new Book("Biography", "large")';

This code is going to be good for creating a new object named someBook and will assign the two different parameters to it as well.

With this adjustment, the object's type is now Biography, while the size is now large.

Whenever you are using the new keyword, the framework of .NET is going to complete two things:

- It will reserve some of the memory for this new object

- It will initialize the object's data members

This is a process that is easy to accomplish, thanks to what is known as the constructor method.

For the code that we took the time to create above, the parameters that we were able to set out will be the exact same parameters that we will use for the class constructor.

This is there to ensure that the object is going to stay where it should in any of the classes that we choose, and it is going to provide an object with characteristics that will make the object behave well in our code.

Releasing the Objects

When we talk about releasing objects, what we mean here is that we can release any of the objects that seem to show up too often in our code, or the ones that are big and may take up too much of the memory and processing power inside of the system without us having to go through and manually destroy them along the way.

You can use one of the systems that are already on the .NET framework to get this to be done, and the CLR system is a great option to rely on as well.

When you are ready to release some of the objects as necessary with the CLR system, the compiler is going to be set up so that it can detect and then automatically release the objects.

The memory that was originally set aside in the code to deal with these objects is going to be free at this time, and you can add in another object or variable to the memory space as long as you take the time to create it as well.

If you want to make sure that the object you are choosing is released, you need to take the time to learn how to destroy the corresponding reference to that object at the same time, or this will not work.

The code that we need to use to make all of this happen includes:

```
someBook = null
```

This process is not going to go through and delete the object, but it will make sure that all references to that object are removed so that the CLR can go through after you are done and perform the deletion for you.

This is a great process to have because it will help to limit the number of issues that occur in your code and can get rid of some of the bugs that show up.

As we can see here, there are a lot of different things that we can put together to help us out with these classes and objects.

When all of these come together, we can make a nice strong code, one that works well and has all of the different parts in it that we need to be successful.

Chapter 7: Defining the C# Classes

In the past chapter, we did touch on these classes a little bit, but mostly in how they are going to relate to our objects and make our codes a bit stronger in that manner.

Now it is time for us to take this a little bit further and really explore these classes.

Part of the benefit of working with the C# language, and the fact that it is seen as an OOP language, is that we can work with these classes and the objects that go with them.

But to ensure that this is all set up properly and that we can actually put things together and get them to work for our needs well, we need to define the classes, call them up, and do a bunch of other actions.

And that is exactly what this chapter is all about.

Working with Our Classes

When it is time to add in one of these classes in the C# language, the class has to be done right.

This is important because it is the part that is going to help us define the types of objects, and the different data types that we will use in that part of the program.

The object is going to help us contain the information that is then going to define the class, which can be seen as a type of container in the code that our object is found inside.

These classes are going to be nice to work with because there is a ton of information that they hold onto and can bring forward whenever we need it.

Not only are they able to hold onto all of those objects that we create, but they can also hold onto any of the information that will describe, both the features and the behavior that comes with these objects as well.

The behavior that we are talking about here is all of the behavior that we want the objects to handle as we execute the code.

When we are working with OOP languages like C#, you will learn why it is so important to work with methods that can get the job done like this.

So, the first thing that we need to spend some time on here is looking through all of the important components that need to show up in our class.

With these classes, there are going to be several components that are nice to work with and should be there to make sure the class behaves.

There are a few different parts that we need to look through at the time of handling the classes as well, including the following:

- Declaration—this is the line that will declare the identifier of the class.
- Body—just like with methods, the classes are going to have a single body.

  You will need to define the body right after you make the declaration.

  The body is the statement, or several statements, that are found between the curly brackets.

  An example of this is:

```
class Example
{
//This is the body of the "Example" class.
}
```

- Constructor—This is the part that will allow you to create a new object. An example of this is:

```
Public Sample()
{
```

```
//Insert what you want to say here.

}
```

- Fields—these are the variables that you will declare within your class.

  The fields are going to contain the values that will represent the exact state of the object they are trying to get to.

- Properties—this part will describe the different attributes of the class.

  Many programmers will write the class properties right inside the field of their chosen object.

- Methods—a method is basically a named block of code that is executable.

  It can complete some tasks and then will allow objects to attain the right behavior.

  It can also execute the right algorithms that are present inside the codes.

When we go through and create some of the codes and the classes that we want to use in this language, remember that we are not able to go through and do any kind of manipulation on the objects that we want to create directly.

Instead, you will need to go through and assign the objects ahead of time so that it is easier to handle some of the manipulations that you want to work with later on without having to worry about the problems as well.

How to Organize Your Classes

The next thing to consider here is that we need to have some organization for the classes that we are handling in the C# language.

There is mainly one big rule that we need to follow to make sure that these classes work.

And this rule is that we need to double-check that our classes have been saved as a .cs file.

This makes them a lot easier for us and the compiler to find so that the code can bring the class out at the right time.

If we are looking at this technically, the C# language can take all of our classes and save them in a program under one big file name, and then the compiler can go through and read that information without running into any errors.

But many programmers like to make sure that their classes stay in individual files because this allows for some ease of use when working on the individual files, and it can help with the organization.

Both methods work, though, so go ahead and pick the one that you like the most.

At this time, we need to understand the topic of a namespace in coding.

This is going to be a set of classes that are related to one another in some manner.

The way that these can relate with each other is going to be based on your code and the situation you put them in, but there should be some sense as to why they relate to one another.

It could be something like their classes, their interfaces, their structure, and even sometimes, the information that is found inside of them.

If you are writing out the code and you would like to add in or create a new namespace in some of the codes that you did in the past, you have to make sure that you work with the directive of "using" to make this easier.

However, it is often better to do this right at the beginning of that part of the code in the first few lines, so that is a good option as well.

Accessing Our Classes

The final topic that we need to take a look at in this guidebook is all about how we can actually access one of our classes in this language.

This language is unique in that it is going to provide us with four modifiers that we can use to help access our classes, and even for us to determine who else is able to access these as well.

These four modifiers are going to include protected, public, private, and internal, and they are going to have the control that is necessary to figure out when the parts can be pulled up, which parts of the code can pull them up, and more.

A bit more about how each of these modifiers works is below:

- Private: This is the modifier that will place some strict restrictions on one of your classes.

  If the class is tagged as a private class, it will not be accessible by the other classes in the code.

  The C# language will use this as the default modifier if you do not place anything else there.

  This can help to avoid problems if you forget to add on that modifier.

- Public: You can also choose to make the class public.

This means that the modifier will tell other classes that they can access this class.

This modifier is going to take away all the limitations about how visible this class is to all the others.

- Internal: If your code has the internal modifier on it, this means that this class is going to be accessible, but only to the files that fall in the same project.
- Protected: This is the modifier that you will use if you would like to prevent a user from accessing the element.

  However, it also allows all the descendant classes to have access to the elements of that class if they need it.

As you can see with this one, all of the elements are going to be able to work in a slightly different manner based on what you are hoping to see happen inside some of your codes.

You can determine if a certain part, or all of it really, needs to be private, or if these can be public for others to see.

You can determine if something is going to be protected or not.

It all depends on the kind of code that you are trying to write out, and what you want to see happen with all of the classes that you create.

There are a lot of great classes that we can create when we work on the C# language, and these classes, along with the objects that go inside of them, are one of the best features that come with this language.

Learning how to work with them and what all they are able to do for some of the codes that we want to write can be pretty amazing, and we can do so many things with these classes along the way.

Chapter 8: How to Create C# Loops

Now that we have a better understanding of how the classes and objects are going to work in some of our codes, it is time for us to dive in a bit and look more at another topic that is going to help our codes come alive in no time.

In many of the OOP languages that we want to spend our time on, you will find that it is possible to work with a type of coding that is simple, can clean up the code, and can make really complex parts of our coding get done in just a few lines, and these are going to be known as the loops.

As we mentioned a bit before, these loops are going to be great to use.

They save us a lot of time and hassle in the process and can ensure that the whole process of writing out codes does not take as long to handle as before.

In this chapter, we are going to take some time to look at what these loops are like, how we are able to create them, and even a few of the options that we have when it comes to using loops for our needs.

Any time that we bring up the idea of loops in any coding language, we can think about it as a method that is used to help us execute a statement, and in some cases, a set of statements; many times over and over again, depending on the results of the condition that we put in place and that we want the loop to be able to evaluate in the first place.

Sometimes, the loop will only go through the iteration a few times, and other times it could go through that iteration many times, depending on how the program works and what we want to get out of it in the process.

In many cases, we are going to find that the loops we want to work with are divided up into two categories.

The first kind is going to be known as the entry controlled loops.

The loops where you are going to have the condition tested at the beginning of the loop are going to be then part of these entry controlled loops.

And these include a few options, including the while loop and the for loop.

In order for us to really see how this is supposed to work, we have to make sure that whatever condition you are testing is going to start showing up at the beginning of the code.

The compiler is going to go through and check the condition that is found in the syntax first, and if this turns out to be true, then it is going to run the loop.

This is going to work well when it comes to most of the loops that we want to work with, but there are some situations where the loop will not run at all with this option because the conditions will not be met.

Now, to help us out here, we need to take a closer look at a few of the loops that will fit into this category.

The first type is going to be known as the while loop.

With this one, the test condition is going to be seen right at the beginning of the loop, and then all of the statements that we are able to work with will be executed until the given condition, which is the Boolean when it comes to these loops, can be satisfied.

When the condition we are working with is seen as false with this one, then the control is going to be out from the while loop, and then the loop will have to completely stop.

Instead, it is going to head on to the next part of the code rather than running the loop at all.

Working with this kind of coding and loop is not that hard to work with.

We are going to take a look at an example of how we are able to handle this in a moment.

Take a look at the syntax and experiment a little bit with it to see how it is going to work.

You can also look for the while part of the code, which is going to tell us where the loop we are working with is going to start.

An example of how we are able to work with the while loop is below:

```
// C# program to illustrate while loop
using System;
class whileLoopDemo
{
  public static void Main()
  {
    int x = 1;
    // Exit when x becomes greater than 4
    while (x <= 4)
    {
      Console.WriteLine("GeeksforGeeks");
      // Increment the value of x for
      // next iteration
      x++;
    }
  }
```

```
}
```

When it comes to creating this kind of loop, one that is set up to write out a certain message three times, we are working with a while loop that told our code only to do this three times and no more.

If we had set up the loop to do this four times, then the condition we are working with would be seen as false, and we would end up with the wrong results here.

This particular code is going to see that we are true when we write it out once because that is below four times.

The same is true as we go up the numbers and have it written out two and then three times.

But when the loop heads on through again, it is going to do that final iteration and sees that if it writes it again, it is going to do it the fourth time and that will not work either.

It is also possible for us to go through and change up some of the terms that we want to do with this kind of loop, and see which statements work the best for your codes here.

You can also get some practice messing around a bit and change up the iterations and more to see if it is still going to work the way that you want.

When you are done experimenting with that part of the code, it is time for us to move on and do some work with the for loop.

This is going to be similar when it comes to the functions that we saw in the while loop, but the syntax is a bit different because the way that this works is different.

The for loops are going to be one of the preferred methods to work with when the number of times that you want the statement of the loop to execute is something that you know ahead of time.

When we are doing the initialization of our loop variable, or the condition that we want to test, and the decrement or the increment of the variable is going to be done with just a single line for the loop, you know that you are working with something that gives us a structure that is shorter and easier to work with for our loop.

And when you run into some problems, or you want to be able to fix some parts of your code, you may find that it is easier for us to format the loops so that they can debug later.

Now, before we get into this for loop a bit more, we need to take a look at a few of the important parts of this process to ensure that the loop is actually going to behave in the manner that we want along the way.

The steps that we can use here include:

1. Initialize the variable we use for the loop:

The expression that controls the loop, also known as the variable, has first to be initialized to get things going.

It is going to be the beginning point that we use with this loop.

A variable that is already declared can be used, or you can declare a local variable in the loop that we are currently in.

2. Add in the condition for testing:

   The second part of this process that we need to take a look at is the condition that we will use for testing.

   This is the part that we are able to use to execute all of the statements that are found in the loop.

   It is going to be used in a ton of situations to help us test out the condition for exiting the loop.

   We need to make sure that it returns a Boolean value or a result that is either true or false.

   When the condition is false, then this loop is ready to end.

3. The decrements and the increments:

   The variable of the loop is either going to be incremented or decremented based on what we are hoping to get out of it, and the control that we place in.

When this is ready to happen in either direction, then we will be able to switch back to our testing conditions to see if things match up or if it is time for the loop to be done at this time.

One thing to note before we go through the process of looking at some of the codings that we want to do with this is that the initialization part is only going to be evaluated just one time before the for loop starts.

If you set this up in the manner that you would really like to see, then this is going to be plenty.

With this in mind, let's take some of the information that we talked about above and add it to the coding to see how this kind of loop is going to work:

```
// C# program to illustrate for a loop.

using System;

class forLoopDemo

{

  public static void Main()

  {

    // for loop begins when x=1
```

```
        // and runs till x <=4
        for (int x = 1; x <= 4; x++)
            Console.WriteLine("GeeksforGeeks");
    }
}
```

As we mentioned before, the two loops that we just went through are going to be known as the entry controlled loops in this language.

But now it is time for us to look at another category of loops that we can use in our codes, and these particular options are going to be known as the exit controlled loops.

The loops in which the testing condition is going to be found near the end of the body of the loop will fit into this kind of category.

One note that we should make with these ones, though, is that with the loops that focus on an exist, you are going to have the loop and its body evaluated at least one time.

The code will go through the loop, and then see the testing conditions to check for it before running through the code again.

These conditions are not going to be found at the beginning of the code.

With this in mind, we are going to look at one of the most common loops that fit into this category, known as the do-while loop.

You will find that there are a lot of times in the C# language when we will want to work with the do-while loop.

You may notice, though, that it shares a few similarities with the while loop that we talked about before.

However, the main difference that shows up between the while loop and the do-while loop is that the do-while loop is set up to check the conditions after they have gone through and executed the statements.

What we mean here is that it is going to do the process of executing our loop one time, and then it will be able to check out the conditions and see whether we have gotten them to be met yet or not, rather than having this all happen in the beginning.

With this in mind, it is time for us to go through and look at some of the work that we are able to do with the syntax of the do-while loop.

These are a good type of loop to work with, and it is going to provide us with a ton of good codes in the process.

In the code below, take some time to see what is going on and what parts show up when we want to create a do-while loop.

```
// C# program to illustrate do-while loop
using System;
class dowhileloopDemo
{
   public static void Main()
   {
      int x = 21;
      do
      {
         // The line will be printed even
         // If the condition is false
         Console.WriteLine("GeeksforGeeks");
         x++;
      }
      while (x < 20);
   }
}
```

Another option that is possible when working on our C# loops is one that is known as the infinite loops.

These are unique, and they are basically the ones that are going to have the test condition not evaluate anything as false at any time.

What this is going to mean for us is that the loop is going to get stuck and will continuously execute the statement that you have there.

You will end up having to bring in some external force to get this loop to stop.

This is usually something that is going to happen when you work on the loop and you forget to add in some of the conditions that are necessary for this to work well.

You need to make sure that you go through this and add in the right conditions from the beginning, and ensure that it is all in the right place so that you don't end up with an infinite loop that you are stuck with along the way.

With this in mind, we need to look through this loop and see what it is able to do.

It is going to look similar to some of the loops that we did above, but you should notice that there are going to be a few differences, which is what will make it one of these infinite loops in the first place.

An example of how you can work with an infinite loop includes:

```
// C# program to demonstrate the infinite loop
using System;
class infiniteLoop
{
   public static void Main()
   {
      // The statement will be printed
      // infinite times
      for(;;)
      Console.WriteLine("This is printed infinite times");
   }
}
```

In some situations, when you write out your codes, you may find that combining together two loops, and sometimes more, is going to be the most helpful to what you want to get done.

If this is true for your code, you want to make sure that you are able to combine the loops and get both to run until they are complete.

This is going to be important in several types of codes that you want to write out, whether we are working with a multiplication table or something simple.

A good example of the coding that you can use to make one of these loops will include the following:

```
// C# program to demonstrate nested loops
using System;
class nestedLoops
{
  public static void Main()
  {
    // loop within loop printing GeeksforGeeks
   for(int i = 2; i < 3; i++)
       for(int j = 1; j < i; j++)
           Console.WriteLine("GeeksforGeeks");
  }
```

```
}
```

And now we are on to the last type of loop that we are able to focus on in this chapter.

And this last loop is going to be known as the continue statement.

This is going to be a useful statement because it is designed to skip on over to the execution part of the loop if a specific condition is met, and then it will move the flow so that it is then on the next part for the updating when we would want.

This one is often hard to explain, so we need to look at some of the codings below to help us get a better idea of how the continue statement is supposed to look, and how it is supposed to work as well:

```
// C# program to demonstrate continue statement
using System;
class demoContinue
{
  public static void Main()
  {
```

```
// GeeksforGeeks is printed only 2 times
// because of continue statement
for(int i = 1; i < 3; i++)
{
   if(i == 2)
    continue;


   Console.WriteLine("GeeksforGeeks");
}
}
```

There are a ton of things that you are able to do when it comes to bringing in these loops and making them work for some of our needs along the way.

Each code that you write is going to be a little bit different from all of the others, so it is always a good thing for us to take some time and learn about these loops, how each one is going to work in some of the codings that we want to create, and how they can save us time while keeping our code nice and organized along the way.

Chapter 9 The Arrays, Lists, and Strings

In this chapter, we are going to take a look at a few of the important parts of working with the C# language to help round out the knowledge that we have been able to discuss so far.

In this chapter, we are going to look at three important parts of our coding language that are similar and kind of go together, so we will put them together.

We are going to work with arrays, lists, and strings; and even though they may seem really similar to one another, they do have some important differences that are able to show up in your code.

The strings, lists, and arrays are going to be important in many of the codes that you decide to write in C#.

And the one that you are going to use will often depend on what you plan to do with your code, and what you are hoping to see the items and the lists that you are making do in the long run as well.

So, with that in mind, let's look at some of the comparisons and differences between the strings, lists, and arrays; some of the coding that you can do with them, and more to help us get started.

Working with the Strings

The first part of this process that we need to spend some of our time on is the strings.

To keep it simple, a string is going to be one of the objects in C# that can have a value of the text.

Internally, the text is going to be something that is stored as a sequential and read-only collection that has objects of char.

There isn't going to be the possibility of a character for null-terminating when we use this kind of string, which means that the string is able to contain any number of embedded null characters as you wish.

Along with this, we need to take the time to look at the fact that the length property that comes with our string is important here, and it can represent the number of char objects that are found in the string.

What this means is that we have to look at the number of char objects that are there, rather than at the Unicode characters when we talk about strings.

If you want to go through and access all of the individual code points that are considered Unicode and are in a particular string, then you need to work with the object that is called StringInfo.

Now, before we can move on from here, we have to take a look at something that is going to show up in some of your codes.

You should notice that there is an object that is known as a string, and then another part that is known as System.String.

Any time that we work with C#, the string keyword is simply an alias that is used for String.

This means that String and string are going to be the same, and you can use any option for naming that you want to do for this to workout.

As we go through this, though, you will find that the string class is unique in that it will provide the programmer with all of the methods that are needed to manipulate, create, and even compare the various types of strings that are in our code.

This language can even overload some of our operators to make the common string operations easier to work with.

Keeping this in order and making sure that we work with strings properly, whether we are using them for operations or not, is important in much of the coding we use.

Now that we have all of this information ready and prepared, it is time for us to take a look at the coding that we can use to first declare, and second, initialize the string that we are hoping to work with.

There are several methods that we can use to make this happen, and we can look at a few of the options below:

```
// Declare without initializing.
string message1;
// Initialize to null.
string message2 = null;
// Initialize as an empty string.
// Use the Empty constant instead of the literal "".
string message3 = System.String.Empty;
// Initialize with a regular string literal.
string oldPath = "c:\\Program Files\\Microsoft Visual Studio 8.0";
// Initialize with a verbatim string literal.
string newPath = @"c:\Program Files\Microsoft Visual Studio 9.0";
// Use System.String if you prefer.
System.String greeting = "Hello World!";
```

```
// In local variables (i.e. within a method body)
// you can use implicit typing.
var temp = "I'm still a strongly-typed System.String!";
// Use a const string to prevent 'message4' from
// being used to store another string value.
const string message4 = "You can't get rid of me!";
// Use the String constructor only when creating
// a string from a char*, char[], or sbyte*. See
// System.String documentation for details.
char[] letters = { 'A', 'B', 'C' };
string alphabet = new string(letters);
```

Creating a List

Next, we are able to take a look at the lists.

These are going to be important to work with when it comes to our goals with the C# language, and they are going to be found in a lot of other options of coding languages as well.

Basically, the list is just an object that will take your variables and hold onto them in a specific order that you want.

The type of variable that the list can store will be defined with a syntax that is pretty generic to start with, but we can go through and add things along the way as we need.

The list and the array are going to seem really similar when we first get started, but you will notice as you get to work with them that there are a few differences that we need to keep in mind.

First, the list is something that can be dynamically sized, but the array has to be in a fixed size that you set in the beginning.

When you are not certain about how many variables you would like to list or how many you need at all, then the list is better because you can make more changes to it.

Besides, when you add items to one of these lists, you can make some changes to them as well.

With a few other options, including the tuple or the array, you can't go through and change the items that are placed inside.

With a list, though, if you feel like you need to change things up and not get them to be so much the same, even though the execution of the program is going to be still something we can mess around with. You will find that the list in this language is something that you can use regularly to get work done in your codes.

You may find that with these lists, you can add in a lot of different items as you need, you can move them around, make some changes, and so much more.

A good way to think about the list is like the one you make before going to the grocery store.

You can write on it a bunch, make some changes, move things off, and more.

This is how the list can work with this language as well.

Ending With the Arrays

In addition to working with the strings and the lists that we mentioned above, it is time for us to take a look at the C# arrays and how these works.

With the array, we can make a group of variables and store them all, as long as these variables are the same data type.

You will be able to declare the array that you would like to work with by specifying the type of its element.

So, if you would like the array to store one of the elements, regardless of the element that we bring up, we would need to specify the object as its type.

Before we take the time to write out a bit of the code that we need to help us create some of the arrays that we want, it is important for us to go a bit more into what an array is, and why this is something that we want to work with overall.

An array is going to come with several properties that we can use, and some of these will include:

1. When we use an array, it may come as either single-dimensional, multidimensional, or jagged.

2. The dimensions and the length that you are going to see with these dimensions in our array are going to be established when you first create the array instance.

These are going to be values that we will not be able to change once we create it, no matter how long we decide to use the instance overall.

3. The default values that we can see with the elements of an array that is considered numerical are going to start with zero, and then when we work with the elements that are part of the reference, these are going to be null.

4. When we are working with an array that is seen as jagged, we need to remember that this is actually an array of arrays.

   This means that all of the different elements that we are going to use are like the reference types, and they will be initialized when we come to null.

5. We also have to remember that the arrays are going to be indexed at zero.

   What this is going to mean for our coding is that the array is going to start from 0 as the first element, and then the last element will be n-1.

6. The different elements that we are able to find in our array can come in as any type that we would like based on our code.

   They can even come in as an array type.

7. The types of arrays that we are working with here are going to be a reference type that we will be able to derive from the abstract base type known as Array.

Now, you will find that there are quite a few times when you work on some of the codes you want to do in C# where you will need to bring in these arrays.

And having a good idea of how to work with them, and what they can do for the codes you want to write, will be important.

That is why it is so important to understand some of the features that we listed above, so we can explore some of the different parts of the code that we can do with these arrays below.

There are several methods that we are able to use when it comes to creating our own arrays in the C# language.

The code that we are going to look at below is helpful because it is set up to help us work with several different arrays, including the jagged array, the multidimensional array, and the single-dimensional array based on the codes that we are working with.

The code that we can do with this one will include the following

```
class TestArraysClass

{

  static void Main()
```

```
{
    // Declare a single-dimensional array.
    int[] array1 = new int[5];
    // Declare and set array element values.
    int[] array2 = new int[] { 1, 3, 5, 7, 9 };
    // Alternative syntax.
    int[] array3 = { 1, 2, 3, 4, 5, 6 };
    // Declare a two-dimensional array.
    int[,] multiDimensionalArray1 = new int[2, 3];
    // Declare and set array element values.
    int[,] multiDimensionalArray2 = { { 1, 2, 3 }, { 4, 5, 6 } };
    // Declare a jagged array.
    int[][] jaggedArray = new int[6][];
    // Set the values of the first array in the jagged array
structure.
    jaggedArray[0] = new int[4] { 1, 2, 3, 4 };
  }
}
```

The strings, lists, and arrays in the C# language can add on a new level to some of the work that we are trying to accomplish, and we need to take the time to learn how they can be added to our codes.

We can see that each one is going to be a little bit different, and it often depends on what we are hoping to get out of the process, and how we want the code to behave as well.

Take some time to look at these three options and learn how they work together, how they are different, and how we can use them in our own codes.

Chapter 10: Tips and Tricks to Get the Most from C#

This guidebook has taken some time to look through all of the different parts of coding that we need to know to utilize the C# language to write some of our own codes.

There are a lot of different aspects that we need to keep in mind when it comes to working on this language, but when we can put it all together, we will find that we can create some great codes and programs in the process.

Even though many of the modern coding languages that are out there have been designed to make programming easier for those who are beginners, there are still several challenges that are going to show up when you first get started.

Learning the proper tips and tricks to help us learn this language and make sure that we can catch on to the different parts quickly and efficiently is going to be so important.

One of the things that a beginner has to remember when they go through this process is that they do need to practice, and they need to learn from their mistakes and from some of the problems that show up in their coding.

Even taking a break is often enough to help you get going on this, and can ensure that you won't burn out and have trouble with the process later on.

This chapter is going to take some time to look at the different parts of the coding that we can do with C# and some of the best tips and suggestions that will ensure we can do as much as possible with some of our own coding choices along the way as well. There is a lot to take in when you first get started with coding in any new language, and it is important to learn how to make this as user-friendly as possible.

Some of the tips and suggestions that you can follow when it comes to working with the C# language includes:

Get Lots of Practice

The first tip that we can follow when it is time to learn the C# language is to get a lot of practice.

There are a ton of codes and suggestions and things to learn about in this guidebook, but if you don't actually open up the compiler with C# and try some of it out, you are never going to gain the skills and more that you need to really make this work for you.

That is why the first rule that we need to follow here is to play around with the code and get as much practice as possible.

With any of the new subjects that we want to explore and learn about in any coding language, the sooner that we can get our hands dirty and start messing around with the code, the faster that we can actually learn some of the concepts that are there.

You can't go through and read the information without using it, and then expect that you will remember that information and be able to utilize the code for your own programs.

You have to actually mess with the code and see how it works.

Now, you will find that the best place for us to get started with this tip is to just open up our C# compiler and start to do some of the codes that we want right away.

Take some of the examples that are in this guidebook and just mess around with them a bit.

Even just by typing them into the compiler to start with is a good step in the right direction, and will ensure that we can get some practice.

You can then work and explore from there to get the right results.

The Fundamentals Are Your Friend

Another thing to consider here is how to learn some of the fundamentals that come with our coding language. Even though it sometimes seems like the fundamentals are going to be too basic to work with, and you may feel like you should just race through them without a thought, it is still important to spend our time learning about how these work.

As easy as they are, they are really important to work with as well.

The better that we can work with these fundamentals, the easier it is for us to start mastering some of the more advanced stuff that is going to show up.

Those programmers who try to get into a programming language and then rush through the beginning parts and do not spend the proper time on some of the fundamentals are going to be the first ones who get stuck when they need to make the transition into some of the advanced material that will come later.

So, before you miss out on some of the first classes that we need and skip through some of the basics that are important in all of this, make sure to learn more about the fundamentals and what we can do with it along the way.

Write it Out

It is normal to want to get started with programming, and just want to open up the compiler and start doing all of the codings there.

And while this is one of the methods to use, sometimes trying it out in a different manner, and writing it by hand rather than trying to type it in all the time is going to be the trick that will help us to get this done.

Bringing out the pen and paper to write out our codes will help.

There are a ton of advances to the computers out there, and there are a lot of benefits to using them.

But sometimes the best way to learn something new is actually to write it out and work from there.

Whether you decide to use some scrap paper, a notebook, a whiteboard, or another option, taking the time to code out everything by hand is going to take more time to work with.

There is the requirement to use more caution, precision, and even intent behind all of the lines of code that you try to write out.

You also are not able to check out the code when writing it like you can on the computer, which forces you to pay more attention.

This method is going to take more time and be really consuming when it is time to get things done.

But it is going to be a great method that helps us go through and become a better developer in the process.

And if you plan to use this through college or for a new job, being able to write out the codes that you are using and utilize this for your needs is going to be so important to the success that you want as well.

The more time and practice that you can give to writing out some of your codes by hand, the better you will get at understanding the coding and all that you can do with it.

It forces the programmer to slow down and actually focus on what they want the codes to do.

And then, you can use this as a way to catch your own mistakes and learn what works best for you and what does not.

Ask for Help

When we first get started with writing out codes in this manner, you may have a ton of grand ideas of how things are going to work and how you will become the greatest code writer of all time.

You may believe that nothing is going to go wrong with this and that you can handle it all in no time at all.

And one of the biggest misconceptions that are going to show up with the work that we want to do here is that we assume we really don't need to get any kind of help with our coding at all.

While it would be awesome to get started with coding in any language, with even C# on our own without any help, we have to face reality a bit and remember that we are going to learn in a faster and more efficient manner when we have the right kind of peer feedback and mentors to help us out with this.

What may seem like an impossible bug to work with, or a topic that seems like it is unlearnable when you do it on your own, you will find that when someone with more experience steps in and can help out, things get a lot easier; and you can actually learn something new.

Whether it is online where you ask for help, or you can find someone who is able to come to you in person and offer advice, you should never be scared to ask someone for help.

All of the programmers who are more advanced right now were, at one time, in the same place as you are now.

And most developers are going to love that they actually get a chance to code again, and will be more than willing to help you out with some of the codings that you would like help with.

Of course, we need to be careful with this and not take advantage of it at all through the process.

The best rule to follow here is to never take more than 20 minutes getting someone to help you figure out something with your code.

And you should not ask for help without spending at least 20 minutes on it ahead of time, trying to learn how it works and what you can do with this as well.

Take Breaks

There are going to be times when you are writing out some of the codes that you want to do in the C# language, and then you get stuck on something.

You spend some time on it, but that just seems to make the whole thing worse.

You keep working and working at it, effectively making the problem worse, or not being able to find the problem at all, and your frustration levels keep going up.

You want to be able to fix the problem and get on with your coding, but you just get angrier, and the codes get messier in the process.

When this happens, and this is something that can happen to everyone, we must take the time to take a break.

This is probably the last thing that we want to worry about when it comes to working with the C# language and some of our codes, but it is going to allow us to take a break from the problem and get some fresh air, or at least do something else for some time.

And often, after you take a break and then come back to it, you will find that the problem, which seemed impossible at the start, is actually really easy to fix.

No one wants to give up when they have put in so much time and effort into this process, but in the long run, it can cut down on the frustration and will ensure that you can fix up your code in no time.

Use the C# Community

One of the neat things that we are going to find when it is time to do our coding in the C# language and more, is that there is a large community of different programmers and developers along the way who can help you out.

These communities are going to include a lot of programmers who have been in all stages of the process.

Some are beginners, some have been in the game for a bit, and some are more advanced.

This is great news for you because it allows us a chance to go through and learn a lot of things.

We can ask questions to those who are in the community.

We can find a lot of the codes that we need to help us work on a variety of programs and learn something new.

And we are able to talk to others about the programming language and meet some great people while asking a lot of questions along the way as well.

It is a good idea for you to go through and make sure that you can really find the community that works for you.

There are a ton of these communities online, and we just need to make sure that we find the one that seems the best for us.

This is a great place to resort back to when there are some problems with your codes or when you would like to get something figured out that is not working out that well to start with for your code.

Utilize the Sample Codes Provided

While this guidebook took some time to show you a few samples of codes to show how all of the different types of coding are supposed to work, it is not enough to build up your understanding just to look over the code.

To help develop a true understanding, you need to take some time to run and tinker with the code to see what it can do.

The more time that you can spend working on the code, the better off you will be along the way.

With the addition of things like instructions and comments, the sample codes that you are going to work with are packaged in a manner that is digestible in an easy manner by the reader.

But you will find that sometimes, these are hard to replicate from scratch.

Reading is not going to be the same thing as understanding, and actually going through the process of writing out some of the code on your own, and then running it, is going to make sure that you can learn how to code much faster than before.

The more that we can spend writing and practicing some of the codes that we find, and then testing these codes out as well, and the more that we can tinker with these as well, the easier the coding language is going to be along the way.

This is a great way to make sure that we are able to learn what is going on, what will not work when we make changes and a lot more in the process.

Just reading the code may work in some cases, and it seems like it is the better option to work with, but it is not going to show us the best way to be efficient to actually create your own programs.

Working with the C# language is a great choice to make.

There are a lot of options that we can focus on, and it is a good option for most of the programs that we want to be able to create.

Even as someone who is brand new to the world of programming and is not used to doing any kind of coding, I will find that the C# language is a good option to work with.

When you are ready to get started with the process of learning a new coding language, you will find that these tips are going to ensure that you can get started on the right foot.

Conclusion

Thank you for making it through to the end of **C# for Beginners,** let's hope it was informative and able to provide you with all of the tools you need to achieve your goals, whatever they may be.

The next step is to get to work on using some of the different codes that we have outlined in this guidebook and take your time to learn more about how this language is going to work for your needs.

If you have decided that the C# language is the right one for you to work with, then you are in good company.

Many programmers throughout the world are going to use this language, and now that you are done with this guidebook, you can join the ranks as well.

There are so much knowledge and information inside this guidebook that we can work with, you will find that this is going to be one of the best options that we are able to utilize when it comes the time to work with the C# language.

We took the time to look at the classes and objects, how to create some of our own codes, how to work with the loops and conditional statements, and so much more.

When all of this can come together and combine, you will find that writing out your own codes is going to be simple and easy, and you can get it done in no time.

This guidebook took the time to help us learn more about the C# language and all that it can do for us.

When you are ready to become a programming master, and ready to make all of this coding work for your needs, make sure to check out this guidebook to help you get started.

Finally, if you found this book useful in any way, a review on Amazon is always appreciated!

All Books published by Julian James McKinnon:

Linux for Beginners: A step-by-step guide to learn architecture, installation, configuration, basic functions, command line and all the essentials of Linux, including manipulating and editing files

Hacking with Kali Linux: A Step by Step Guide with Tips and Tricks to Help You Become an Expert Hacker, to Create Your Key Logger, to Create a Man in the Middle Attack and Map Out Your Own Attacks

Hacking for Beginners: A Step by Step Guide to Learn How to Hack Websites, Smartphones, Wireless Networks, Work with Social Engineering, Complete a Penetration Test, and Keep Your Computer Safe

C# For Beginners: A Step-by-Step Guide to Learn C#, Microsoft's Popular Programming Language

C++ for Beginners: A Step-by-Step Guide to Learn, in an Easy Way, the Fundamentals of C++ Programming Language with Practical Examples

SQL For Beginners: A Step-by-Step Guide to Learn SQL (Structured Query Language) from Installation to Database Management and Database Administration

Python Programming for Beginners: A Step-by-Step Guide to Learn one of the Most Popular and Easy Programming Languages. Learn Basic Python Coding Fast with Examples and Tips

Data Science with Python: The Ultimate Step-by-Step Guide for Beginners to Learn Python for Data Science

Arduino: Learn how to Create Interactive Electronic Objects, Setting up your Board, Discover how Coding Works, Create your Circuit plus all the essentials of Arduino Programming (For Beginners)

Raspberry Pi: A Step-by-Step Guide for Beginners to Learn all the essentials of Raspberry Pi and create simple Hardware Projects like an Arcade Box or turning your Device Into a Phone

www.ingramcontent.com/pod-product-compliance
Lightning Source LLC
Chambersburg PA
CBHW071410210526
45465CB00001B/325